Faithful Servant Series
Meditations for Vestry Members

MEDITATIONS FOR
VESTRY MEMBERS

COLLEEN McMAHON
CHRISTOPHER L. WEBBER, SERIES EDITOR

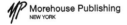

Morehouse Publishing
NEW YORK

FAITHFUL
SERVANT
Series

Unless otherwise noted, the Scripture quotations contained herein are from the New Revised Standard Version Bible, copyright © 1989 by the Division of Christian Education of the National Council of Churches of Christ in the U.S.A. Used by permission. All rights reserved.

Morehouse Publishing, 19 East 34th Street, New York, NY 10016

Morehouse Publishing is an imprint of Church Publishing Incorporated.

Library of Congress Cataloging-in-Publication Data

McMahon, Colleen, 1951-
    Meditations for vestry members / Colleen McMahon.
        p. cm. — (Faithful servant series)
    Includes bibliographical references.
    ISBN 978-0-8192-1789-9 (PBK.)
    1. Church officers—Prayer-books and devotions—English.
2. Episcopal Church—Government—Meditations. I. Title.
II. Series.
BX5967.5.M28 1999   242'.69—dc21

                                98-55384
                                CIP

Passages marked The Book of Common Prayer (BCP) are from the 1979 version.

ISBN 978-0-8192-2861-1 (ebook)

Contents

————"You Were Chosen"————

Were you chosen to read this book? Perhaps it was given to you in a public ceremony or maybe it was handed to you with a quiet "you might like to look at this" Maybe, on the other hand, it reached out to you in a bookstore and said, "Buy me!" Many books choose us in such ways and this book is likelier to have done so than most. But however this book came to you, it almost certainly happened because you have also been chosen for a ministry in the church or for church membership. Perhaps you hadn't considered this as being chosen; you thought you decided for yourself. But no, you were chosen. God acted first, and now you are where you are because God took that initiative.

God acts first—the Bible is very clear about that and God acts to choose us because God loves us. And who is this God who seeks us in so many ways, who calls us from our familiar and comfortable places and moves us into new parishes and new roles? Christians have been seeking answers to that question for a long time.

Part of the answer can be found within the church. We come to know God better by serving as church members and in church ministries. God is present with us and in others all around us as we worship and serve.

But there is always more, and God never forces a way into our hearts. Rather, God waits for us to be quiet and open to a deeper relationship.

And that's what this book is about. This is not simply a book to read but to use, in the hope that you will set aside some time every day for prayer and the Bible—and for this book. So give yourself time not only to read but to consider, to think about, to meditate on what you have read. The writers of these short meditations have been where you are, thought about their experiences deeply, and come to know God better. Our prayer is that through their words and experience and your reflection on them, you will continue to grow in knowledge and love—and faithful service—of this loving, seeking God.

— Christopher L. Webber
    Series Editor

——Ad Majorem Dei Gloriam——

Six months ago, I could not have imagined writing this book. That I have actually done it is cause for giving thanks—especially to all the wonderful people who helped me give birth to it.

First and foremost, I thank Chris Webber, who had the off-the-wall idea that a layperson who had actually served on a vestry should write this volume, and who challenged me to be the one to do it. A job I was reluctant to undertake has turned out to be a resurrection experience.

I cast far and wide for passages that might yield helpful meditations, and a number of friends threw fish into my net. I am grateful to the Rt. Rev. Richard F. Grein, Rev. Dr. Roger E. Ferlo, Rev. Charles J. ("Chad") Minifie, Rev. John Osgood, Rev. Joel E. A. Novey, Rev. S. Elizabeth Searle, George Wade, Esq., and Rev. Nicholson B. White for their ideas. Special thanks to John and Liz, who repeatedly helped me out by serving as my human concordances, and to Chad, who read the manuscript and made some excellent suggestions—a task that surely qualifies as above and beyond a rector's obligations. I rejoice in the vestries, past and present, of Christ Church, Bronxville, New York, who shaped so much of my thinking on this topic, and whose deeds and peccadillos crop up in the text from time to time. I remember especially two fellow travelers on the vestry journey: Sue Garrett, who died shortly before I began to write, and Bess Robinson, who passed away just as I finished. I was enriched by serving with them both.

Maria Poliseno improved mightily on my primitive word-processing skills. My husband, Frank Sica, who has always wanted me to write a book, cheered me on, even though this is not the Grishamesque potboiler he had in mind. Bless you both.

There are many people to whom I could dedicate this book, but I would be remiss if I did not acknowledge the influence of three special people who played key roles in the development of my sense of personal ministry. Since my relationship with each of them resulted—directly or indirectly—from my vestry experience, the dedication is doubly appropriate. So I offer this book, with love and gratitude, to Bob Willing, who showed me why; Hondi Brasco, who told me what; and Pierre Wolff, who taught me how.

─────── Introduction ───────

I have to begin with a confession.

I resigned from my parish vestry rather than serve out my second term. The reason was spiritual and emotional exhaustion. I was elected in a period of crisis, conflict, and factionalism in our parish. Four often agonizing years later, crisis, conflict, and factionalism were still high on our agenda. I concluded that being on the vestry was retarding my growth in God, not enhancing it. In fact, I was starting to hate my church. So I quit. At that time, and for a long time thereafter, I did not remember anything about my vestry experience as either happy or beneficial.

You may well wonder why I should write a book of meditations for vestry members. I wondered the same thing when I was asked (by the person who was my rector during most of those four years) to take on this assignment. Chris Webber's out-of-the-blue request forced me to reevaluate what I had gotten out of my time as a vestry member, and what I might have gotten out of it had things been different.

When I thought about it, I realized that most of the time I loved being on the vestry. The folks who sat around the table were good people, and for the most part, our joint and several intentions were good, too. We shared some tough times, but we shared a lot of laughs as well. We agonized over what we could not accomplish, but we actually accomplished quite a bit, and we laid the foundation for a better future in less contentious times. We took our licks, sometimes from parishioners who were not on the vestry and sometimes from each other. But we gave as good as we got, and we mostly shook hands when our meetings were over.

I realized as well that my years on the vestry had been a time of extraordinary spiritual growth. In fact, I met the three people who would have the most profound influence on my spiritual development because of my vestry membership. The priest who served as our crisis consultant recognized that I was on the verge of a conversion experience and gently pushed me toward it. The woman who sat next to me at meetings became my closest spiritual friend and confidante. She introduced me to the retreat master who became my spiritual guide. None of those relationships would have come about had I not been on our vestry, and I believe I was more open to them because I was actively engaged with the church. What a treasure trove of spiritual riches I gained as a result!

Being on the vestry also seemed to make me more aware of other venues—in our parish and in the wider world—where I could do ministry. I don't think it's an accident that I became much more active in our parish choir, our women's service group, and the Diocese of New York while serving on the vestry. I also began to understand that my work in the law was vocational as well as occupational. Being a steward within my own little corner of the Episcopal Church sensitized me to the possibilities for stewardship elsewhere.

Finally, I realized that there was something to be said for exploring through prayer and meditation the darker side of vestry life, which I experienced in abundance. We are shortsighted if we don't acknowledge that vestry service can have a considerable spiritual downside. Members bring their negative attitudes as well as their positive talents to the vestry and some folks act out their frustrations in that meeting room. No vestry is immune to conflict, anger, factionalism, power struggles, and other downright unchristian behavior. There were times when I wondered if God was anywhere near our meetings. I know that's not a unique feeling among vestry members. It is indeed unfortunate that I felt I had to leave the vestry in order to exorcize those particular demons. Countless others have done the same. If we had had a book like this one, however, perhaps that would not have been necessary.

So I guess I do bring something to this exercise: a pretty well-rounded understanding of what the vestry experience can be. I hope I can translate that understanding into a tool that helps you get through it with grace and good humor.

I have organized these meditations around five themes that you will encounter as you live out your vestry term: the call to service, the job to be done, getting along with each other and the rest of the parish, the importance of prayer, and life after you leave the vestry. They can be used for individual devotions or group prayer. But they are only a jumping-off point. Whether you only ruminate on them alone or with others, they were written to begin discussion, not to be the last word. If some of my musings ring a bell with you or help you to relate your own vestry experience to a particular passage of Scripture, then this book will have served its purpose.

The Call

Come, follow me

Matthew 4:18-22, Mark 1:16-20,
Luke 5:1-11, John 1:35-51

Long before he acquired a reputation for preaching great sermons or doing miraculous deeds, Jesus convinced some perfectly ordinary folks to put their lives on hold and do ministry with him. The Gospels offer different explanations for their seemingly irrational behavior. In John, the disciples immediately recognized Jesus as the Messiah, which certainly made their decision to follow him plausible. Luke's apostles were the beneficiaries of a bona fide miracle; who wouldn't follow a fellow who filled your nets with fish and your pockets with money? By contrast, Matthew and Mark can suggest no reason at all why Peter, Andrew, James, and John decided to walk away from life as they knew it. The only common element in all four Gospels is that Jesus called people out of everyday life to help him, and they answered yes.

When you agreed to serve on the vestry you too answered a call. It came from your rector or wardens or nominating committee, of course, but they were standing in for God. Joining the vestry is a way of responding to God's call by serving a community (your parish church) that nurtures and sustains you in important ways.

Like the disciples in the various Gospels, people say yes when God calls them to the vestry for different reasons, or for no apparent reason. For some, it is a matter of principle, of giving back to the community. For others, it is a form of worship, of putting faith into practice. Maybe you had an encounter with the Lord that knocked you on your rear and inspired you to dedicate some of your time to God's service. Maybe you just decided it was your turn. Or maybe you don't know why you said yes; I imagine that most folks wake up the morning after they agree to stand for election and wonder what hit them. But as the Gospels put different spins on it, I guess we can conclude that God probably doesn't much care why people who are called say yes—only that they do.

Of course, responding to this call is not without cost. Like all calls from God, vestry service will take you away from things you think you ought to be doing, whether that is spending more time on the job, taking care of the home, or doing some good deed for your community or worthy organization. Like all calls from God, it will make demands on you that will not necessarily be understood by your boss, co-workers, family, or friends. Like all calls from God, it will not get you ahead in the world—at least not in the sense that the world understands getting ahead. And like all calls from

God, it will lead to stresses that you could easily avoid just by saying no.

It was ever thus. The apostles' yes led to results that far exceed anything your parish will ask of you; they endured career changes, endless travel, relocation, imprisonment, even death. They could not have foreseen paying such a high price at the outset, of course, but in the end the cost must have seemed insignificant compared with what they received in exchange: a chance to see their God more clearly, love him more dearly, and follow him more nearly every day of their lives.

Your rewards may seem tame by comparison, but they can be as life-transforming as anything that happened to the Twelve. As the myriad details of congregational life unfold before you, you will discover what a complex organization your parish church is. You will catch glimpses of God in the mundane details of its administration, like folding the newsletter or fixing the broken stair rail. And you will find new uses for your talents—or perhaps discover talents you didn't know you had. If you think about it, all those things happened to Jesus' first helpers, too.

So as you embark on this new adventure, rejoice in your yes. You may suspect from time to time that God has pulled a fast one on you—but then again, don't we all?

All things come of thee, O Lord, and of thine own have we given thee

1 Chronicles 29:14

The best sermon I ever heard about the apostles made a point that is often overlooked. The people who were asked to follow the itinerant preacher Jesus did not lack for other things to do. Forget all that "happy, simple fisherfolk" imagery of song and story; it's a lovely myth, but it doesn't mesh with the Gospels' description of the Twelve. Peter and Andrew and the Zebedee brothers were men of means, with their own boats and their own nets. James and John also had a father who apparently couldn't look after himself and hired hands who were paid to work the boats and look out for dad. Then there was the sickly mother-in-law, which implies that there was a wife, and where there are wives, quite possibly there are children also. Matthew was a public official, a tax collector, responsible to the state. Simon, and perhaps Judas, were involved in local politics. In other words, most of the people Jesus called into a life of ministry had built careers and taken on other responsibilities. They needed to earn a living and be there for their families or friends or causes. It's shocking that they did not respond to Jesus' invitation by saying, "Look, I'd really like to follow you, but I'm much too busy right now. Maybe some other time, OK?"

But they didn't. They followed him, just as he asked. They found the time.

There will be times when it will be terribly inconvenient to be on the vestry. There will be times when you'll have to choose between attending a baseball game or the vestry retreat, between spending Saturday night at a restaurant with friends or in the undercroft with the furnace repairman, or between finishing a special project or your Every Member Canvass visits. When those moments come, it helps to remember what you really agreed to do when you said yes to your congregation's call. You agreed to give back to God some of what God has so generously given to you. King David said it best: "All this abundance that we have provided for building you a house for your holy name comes from your hand and is all your own" (1 Chron. 29:16).

Now here's the strange part. The abundance you are being asked to provide for the building of God's house in your community is time—the time to go to meetings and give advice over the phone and be responsible for part of your parish's life. That probably strikes you as funny. Time is not an abundant commodity for most of us these days. Vestry service is just one more responsibility that will take time most of us don't believe we have.

But time, like everything else, is a gift from God. Remember that God operates out of a model of abundance—not scarcity—and never gives less than generously. Therefore, if you are truly called to vestry ministry, the time to do the job will be given to you, even if it doesn't seem so when you look at your calendar.

That seems to be the way it worked with the Twelve. They spent plenty of time on the road in the service of their Lord. But they also found time to keep their boats and equipment in working order; otherwise, there could never have been any midnight rides across the lake or unproductive fishing trips that ended with net-breaking catches.

How could they possibly fit it all in? God alone knows. But they managed. God alone knows how you will manage all the things you'll have to juggle in order to fit in your new responsibilities. But you will. If you say yes, God will give you the time—so you can give it back.

Take up the whole armor of God

Ephesians 6:11-17

According to the dictionary, the word "vestry" derives from the Latin "vestire," which means "to clothe" The word has two definitions. One is the elected group of advisers in an Anglican church. The other is the room where we keep vestments, which are, of course, clothes. I don't know why vestries bear the same name as robing rooms—unless that's where the lay council of advice in some English parish first held its meetings—but from time to time we ought to go back to our roots and see what we can learn from the image of vesting, or clothing, ourselves.

There's a kernel of truth in the old saying "clothes make the man" (or "the person," in today's parlance). Particular clothing is appropriate to particular situations. So what outfit makes a vestry member? Well, given what you're getting into, you could do worse than to put on the whole armor of God.

I don't think St. Paul attended a vestry meeting before he wrote to his friends in Ephesus, but there must have been something quite similar to a vestry in the Early Church, because he really hit the nail on the head when he described what most vestries seem to encounter. "For our struggle is not against the enemies of blood and flesh," he wrote, "but against... the cosmic powers of this present darkness, against the spiritual forces of evil in the heavenly places" (Eph. 6:12). What metaphor could possibly be more apt? Here you have a group of well-intentioned folks who love God and their church and only want to make a heavenly place even more so. And what do they come up against? The cosmic powers of darkness and the spiritual forces of evil—not carrying pitchforks, but spewing fire and brimstone about the budget, parish priorities, or change versus the status quo. It's amazing how riled up people can get over which gets fixed first, the plumbing or the roof. Or whether it's better to hold two services, at 9:00 and 11:00, or one at 10:00. Or how to spend old Mrs. Smith's bequest. Or what the mission statement ought to say. Things that have almost no significance in and of themselves can bring out the worst in people if the circumstances are right. When the vestry becomes a venue for fulfilling our devilish need for power and control, the heavenly place turns into a breeding ground for pride, anger, and envy. A good suit of armor sounds pretty appealing when you're up against such deadly sins.

But in a heavenly place, not just any old suit of armor will do. It has to be the armor of God. The belt of truth, so you can keep your shirt on. The breastplate of righteousness and the shield of faith, so the flaming arrows of pride won't pierce your heart and poison your soul. Carefully crafted boots, so you can stand up for what you believe without stepping on anyone else in the process.

Above all, you need to wield the sword of the Spirit, the Word of God, which is love. No matter what happens or how often you find yourself on the losing side of an issue, no matter how many times the Altar Guild ladies, the music director, or the members of last year's vestry complain about your decisions, the weapon you fight back with is love. You listen with love. You try to persuade with love. You poke and prod, you thrust and parry with love, remembering that the only reason you have a church to take care of and fight for is that once upon a time love really did conquer all. Trust that the only weapon Jesus ever held will protect you from your enemies, and from yourself as well. Pick it up and feel its power. Then put it in your scabbard and go back into the fray.

Take nothing for your journey

The last time I watched my favorite Jesus movie, Franco Zeffirelli's *Jesus of Nazareth*, I noticed that Judas and the other eleven apostles were following Jesus for very different reasons. Peter, James, John, and the rest, are obviously fascinated by this man they call Master. They don't really understand him—quite the opposite, in fact—but they love him so much that they try to figure out what he is up to. In so doing, they absorb more and more of his message. Eventually, it becomes their message, too.

Zeffirelli's Judas latches onto Jesus for his own reasons. He is looking for a charismatic figure to lead a revolution against the Romans. When he meets a very charismatic man with leadership potential, he projects his own desires onto everything Jesus says and does. Judas is also fascinated by his rabbi, but he is not trying to tune into Jesus' agenda; he wants Jesus to tune into his agenda. You know how the story ends: Judas and his agenda die, while the eleven sit huddled in a tiny room, frightened but strangely transformed and ready to carry on the Lord's work. Jesus lives.

Ideally, people who join vestries want only to serve their Lord in whatever way God requires of them. If everyone held to that purest of motives, vestries would be remarkably productive. But sometimes we come to this holy work with our own agendas. For the most part, these are benign and meant for good—wanting to improve the Sunday school, for example, or wanting to refocus the parish's attention on new member programs or outreach. But any one member's priority may not be ideal for the parish as a whole. That is why we ask a *group* of committed Christians to discern, corporately, God's plea for the congregation. If it seems to the group that what one member wants is not what God wants for the parish, things can get a little dicey, just as they did between Jesus and Judas. Even greater problems are created when we have secret motives—sometimes secret even from ourselves—like the need for power, the desire to feel superior or be "in the know," or even the chance for revenge.

Unfortunately, few of us take the time to dissect our motives before we embark on vestry service. That's too bad, because they can get in the way of effective discipleship to our congregations, just as Judas' agenda, which seemed to him noble and important, prevented him from focusing on what Jesus was trying to do.

My rector has an interesting way of teasing out vestry members' secret motivations. He likes to start the annual vestry retreat with a meditation on the exhortation Jesus delivered to his disciples before he sent them out, two by two, to spread the gospel. "Don't take a lot of baggage" Jesus told them. "No staff. No extra clothes, no provisions, and no money. Travel light." Jesus sent his friends out armed with nothing but the Word. Yet they enjoyed remarkable success on their travels; they "went through the villages, bringing the good news and curing diseases everywhere" (Luke 9:6). The rector asks the members to inventory all the baggage they are bringing with them to the vestry and to write down anything they may be carrying over and above what Jesus said was necessary. At the concluding Eucharist, he invites them to hand in their lists and lay all that excess baggage on the altar.

Humans are motivational animals, and it's tough to set those motives aside, especially if we're not fully conscious of them. But Jesus knew that the only right agenda was God's agenda. It's hard to discern what that might be if we are busy meditating on our own goals and plans. True disciples of Jesus heed their Master's warning and travel light as they carry out their ministry. What baggage should you lay aside before you embark on your vestry?

Now there are varieties of gifts, but the same Spirit

1 Corinthians 12

The twelfth chapter of Paul's First Letter to the Corinthians is an essay on the importance of diversity in the Christian church. First directly and then meta-phorically, Paul tells his Corinthian converts that each of them adds something valuable and necessary to the Christian community. What this one or that one brings to the table may not be immediately apparent, especially when judged by the world's standards. But just as no part of the body is superfluous, no one's spiritual gifts are unimportant to the work of the congregation.

As you look around the vestry table, some members' gifts will be obvious. That's because the parish wants them to apply their secular talents to the work of the parish. The accountant can analyze the balance sheet; the teacher may have some ideas for improving Sunday school; the lawyer should alert everyone to potential lia-bilities; the roofer is a natural for building maintenance; the hostess with the mostest ensures that the congrega-tion puts its best foot forward at coffee hour. Applying one's worldly talents to the Lord's service transforms them into spiritual gifts. No parish can afford to over-look such gifts as it identifies potential vestry members.

But other, less obvious talents are equally important for an effective vestry, and it is a fortunate congregation indeed that recognizes and values them for the blessing they are. When I think about people who manifest these special gifts the first person who comes to mind is Susanne Garrett. Sue was a librarian by profession. She was soft-spoken and bookish. In a parish full of highly opinionated, take-charge, Type A personalities, Sue did not initially impress one as a key player. She sat quietly at one end of the table and knit throughout our meetings. A half-smile played about her lips all the time, and her needles never stopped clicking, even as heated arguments raged around her. Sue seldom spoke, but when she made an observation it was generally witty (the woman had a wicked sense of humor) and always wise. More often than not, she succeeded in changing the tenor of the debate simply by calling our attention to the spiritual side of whatever we were doing. Without her calming presence in a time of crisis and dissension, I am convinced that the rest of us—who behaved more like what secular society imagines leaders to be—would have accomplished very little.

What gifts did Sue bring to the table? Her serenity, her centeredness, and her conviction about who and what were truly important. These qualities may not cry leadership in late twentieth-century America, but they passed what Paul tells us is the true test of whether we are manifesting gifts of the Spirit—they worked "for the common good" (1 Cor. 12:7). If I can expand a tad on Paul's wonderful metaphor about the parts of the body,

I would say Sue was our conscience; and because we had a conscience, the other parts of our vestry were better able to work together for the benefit of the parish as a whole, despite some very different attitudes and opinions within the group.

As you look around your own vestry table, you may wonder whether certain people can make a meaningful contribution to the work you need to do. Or perhaps you question whether you yourself have something important to offer. The answer to both questions is yes. To each is given some manifestation of the Spirit. Look at yourself and each other again, this time with what Paul called "the eyes of your heart" (Eph. 1:18). Don't focus on the obvious. Try to see what God might see in each of you, and how he might use you to accomplish the work of your parish.

The Job

*The greatest among you must become like the
youngest, and the leader like one who serves*

Luke 22:24-28

I don't know what you imagined vestry service would be
like, but if you are reading this book, you probably know
you were wrong. The vestry of an Episcopal Church is
not a broadly empowered legislative body, at least not
as envisaged by our Church's Constitution and Canons.
It is the board of directors of a charitable corporation,
namely your parish church. For legal purposes, you own
the worldly goods of the corporation, holding them in
trust for the present and future members of that corporation. You are responsible for raising money to sustain
your congregation, its clergy, and its work, and you are
also responsible for deciding how that money will be
spent. Your actions have legal consequences, and you are
held to the standards of a fiduciary or trustee under the
law. However, if your congregation has a rector, many
of what might otherwise be your powers are circum-
scribed by prerogatives that our Church (unlike most
other Christian denominations) gives to a tenured class
of clergy. If your congregation is headed by a vicar or
priest-in-charge, as many are these days, it may surprise

you to learn that you are subject to a pretty fair degree of control from the bishop of your diocese. Either way, you are not a free agent. Yet the legal and moral responsibility for an awful lot of stuff gets dumped in your lap.

If this does not sound inspiring to you, rest assured you are not the first person to react that way. The vestry's ministry is to take care of the church's temporal things. The challenge is to discover the spiritual underpinnings of such worldly work.

One way to do that is to focus on what it means to be a servant leader. Leaders generally set the agenda and exhort others to do their bidding. Servants, by contrast, do what needs to be done, which is generally the grunt work or the dirtiest jobs—the kinds of things the traditional leader feels he or she is above doing. Jesus' greatest accomplishment was pointing out and living out the seeming contradiction between servanthood and leadership. Now God asks you to do the same.

Vestry members are generally thought of as the leaders in their congregations, yet the work you are called to do comprises the least glamorous and most back-breaking tasks that have to be performed for a congregation—the jobs no one else wants to do, the problems no one else wants to tackle. There is an exquisite irony in this. But exquisite ironies stand squarely at the center of Christianity: The weak are strong, the poor are rich, death brings life. So servant leadership is in the best Christian tradition.

Vestries can only benefit from returning over and over again to the image of Jesus washing the feet of his apostles. It perfectly encapsulates who you are, what your job is, and what your attitude toward it ought to be. At the Last Supper, the One who by rights should have been waited on by others not only took care of their needs, but did so in a way that the disciples themselves would have disdained—he washed their filthy feet, a task deemed fitting only for a slave. And when Peter, out of respect, tried to stop Jesus from demeaning himself in this way, his Lord replied, "Unless I wash you, you have no share with me" (John 13:8). Jesus' meaning is clear—loving service is not only the leader's task, but also the essence of the relationship between those who lead and those who are led.

You are the ones who are called to do the unappealing, behind-the-scenes work of keeping the parish afloat. If you can do that job with joy and gratitude for the chance to be of service in this particular way, you will be true Christian leaders.

Woe to you when all speak well of you, for that is what their ancestors did to the false prophets

Luke 6:26

The other day, I was talking to a friend who serves as a warden in my parish. We were discussing a survey the vestry had commissioned prior to commencing our capital campaign. To our mutual consternation, the results revealed little support among potential donors for contributing to outreach in the wider community. When I expressed my dismay, he said, "Well, it's too bad, but don't worry. When we set the goals for the campaign, we'll do the right thing. After all, this is a church, not a democracy."

Throughout the Judeo-Christian tradition, leadership has devolved onto prophets—not fortune-tellers, but fearless men and women who have tried to discern the will of God and proclaim it to the community. This did not make them popular. To the contrary, those who tried to point out God's way were despised and rejected. The Israelites turned on Moses as soon as they got hungry. Elijah spent most of his life dodging the wrath of Ahab and Jezebel. Jeremiah was left to die at the bottom of a dry well. Then there were the great leaders of the New Covenant: Jesus, John the Baptist, Peter, Paul. Look what happened to them. Yet these prophets are our tradition's models for leadership.

For the most part, the prophets were people of vision rather than people of wealth or power or prestige in the community. (In fact, power, prestige, and popularity were almost always a recipe for poor leadership among God's chosen.) And they were reluctant to be prophets, every one of them. But God calls prophets in every generation, and those who are chosen generally rise to the occasion.

Which brings me back to my conversation with my friend. It would have been easy enough for him and his vestry to throw up their hands and say, "Look, we know outreach is important, but we took a poll and people are just not interested in it. So let's just fix up the building; we know we can raise the money for that. Outreach will have to wait." But the leaders of the parish recognized that outreach had to be in the budget or we would be a sorry example of a Christian community. So they decided to exercise prophetic leadership in the best Judeo-Christian tradition. Their final statement of goals included a tithe of the proceeds for the poor and the outcast, even though it meant spending less on needed parish projects. Like the prophets of old, they discerned the will of God and proclaimed it; they pointed the way, regardless of popular sentiment. I'm sure they took some heat for their decision. Real leaders always do.

When you are elected to the vestry, you never know where you will be called upon to exercise prophetic leadership. But you are kidding yourself if you think it will never happen. Perhaps you will have to mediate a paralyzing dispute among parish factions over the fate of your rector. Perhaps you will have to stand up to local politicians who pander for votes by attacking your soup kitchen as an impediment to urban renewal. Perhaps you will have to say no to a much-needed donation that comes with too many strings attached. I know vestries that have found themselves in these situations, each of which called for truly prophetic leadership, none of which could be resolved without angering somebody. Perhaps you are facing such a conflict right now. If so, remember that God has raised you up to be prophets for your parish. Your job is to discern God's will and point the way, whether it makes you popular with your fellow congregants or not. Woe to you if all you care about is the folks in the pew speaking well of you.

The sower went out to sow his seed

Mark 4:1-20

The sower went out to sow his seed. Three quarters of
what he planted was lost to one disaster or another. The
labor was great, but the harvest was on the lean side. A
real farmer couldn't operate for long with a crop yield
of only 25 percent. There's no profit in it.

But Jesus' sower just keeps sowing along. The birds
eat some of his seed, some can't take root in the rocky
soil, and some is choked by thorns. None of that matters. He plants it all and harvests whatever that planting
yields, and he does it again the next year, and the next.
The sower of the parable is not discouraged by his fail-
ures; he glories in his successes and uses their fruits to
sow again.

Most of us join the vestry full of ideas for how to
improve some aspect or another of parish life. Few
things are as discouraging as not having those ideas pan
out. Sometimes we run into the familiar attitude, "We've
always done it this way." Sometimes ideas conflict, and
someone else's wins. Sometimes we try one out and, for
whatever reason, it just doesn't work.

One year while I was on the vestry, I ran the annual
pledge drive. It was not an enviable job; our income had
been declining year by year for almost a decade, and we
were dipping into our modest endowment to make ends
meet. Trying to come up with a new angle to increase

donations, I had what I thought was a terribly bright idea. Three months before the pledge cards went out, we would have an Every Member Canvass, not to ask for money, but to ask people what they liked and disliked about the parish. A marketing professional who attended our church drafted a questionnaire to elicit opinions about everything from the time of our services to how people would describe the parish to others. Every warden and vestry member was asked to bring the questionnaire to parishioners' homes and personally solicit comments on parish affairs. All this was carried out with lots of whoopla; there were plenty of announcements in the newsletter, and cards went out telling people to expect a visit soon.

What happened was predictable. Only a few canvassers carried out their assignment as planned. Some vestry members were too busy to pay visits, so they just placed phone calls or put the questionnaires in the mail. A few never got around to contacting their assigned parishioners at all. Some parishioners were offended by the combination of market research and religion. Those who never heard from anyone concluded that their opinions were not valued. As I recall, we had only about 25 percent participation in our "Every" Member Canvass. Pledges didn't go down, but they didn't go up either. Many people thought the whole project was a public relations disaster.

But what a harvest we gathered from those who responded! This demographically diverse group exhibited a surprising degree of unanimity about what in our church was precious to them. There was also a surprising degree of unanimity about what the respondents disliked; as a result, we were able to make some immediate recommendations for popular changes. More important, when our rector retired unexpectedly a few months later, we had in hand some extremely useful data for our parish profile.

My bright idea did not work out as I hoped it would. Some of yours won't either. But that's not a reason to stop having them. Sometimes what looks like a failure turns out to have seeds of success—witness the serendipitous usefulness of our Not-Quite-Every Member Canvass. And sometimes an idea that people are skeptical about catches hold and takes off. You just never know.

One thing is certain: If you stop sowing, there will be nothing to reap. So keep throwing out those ideas and let your parish's version of nature take its course. It's hard to predict which ideas will take root, but some of them will. And they will bear fruit thirty- and sixty- and a hundred-fold. That's a promise.

If these were silent, the very stones would cry out

Luke 19:40

At lunch the other day, a friend who serves as rector of a particularly vibrant parish was lamenting a common problem: "My new vestry members are all excited when they're elected, and they become so disillusioned once they figure out that it's really about the plumbing."

My friend was right about that. Chief among a vestry's few canonical responsibilities is serving as the agent and legal representative of the parish in all matters concerning corporate property. In plain English, that means the vestry holds the property of the parish in trust for the congregation and takes care of it. Your job is to fix the leaks and repoint the steeple, and to make sure the stairs are safe, the paint is fresh, and the fire extinguisher is full. You watch out for the parish's temporalities, its earthly things. On the face of it, vestry service does not seem to afford a good vehicle for spiritual growth.

But the temporalities of a church are sacred. Our churches were built for the same reason the princes and artisans of the Middle Ages built their soaring cathedrals and abbeys—to give glory to God. The buildings themselves are acts of worship. Some are made of cedar and bronze and costly stone, like Solomon's Temple; others are small prefabricated chapels without elaborate adornment. But all of them represent the best that their builders had to give. To have the care and custody of such space is an awesome thing, a holy calling.

If you want to know just how holy, go and spend some time alone in your church. The praise and thanks, the hopes and fears, the joys and sorrows, the sins and repentance of those who have worshiped there are as much a part of the fabric of the building as are the brick and mortar. The walls have soaked up all the prayers ever prayed inside them. Stand quietly in the nave and let those prayers flow over you. Summon the memory of a child's christening, a friend's wedding, a father's funeral—all the holy laughter and holy tears that have attended life's rites of passages through generations. Recall the sound of a hundred hymns and anthems swelling in your ears. Watch the light stream in through the stained glass; see the candles flicker as the gospel procession marches by. Remember how it feels when the Host touches your lips and your heart floods with grace. Wander into the Sunday school and imagine all the little ones who met Jesus for the first time at those tiny tables. Taste the coffee and donuts and the fellowship that fill the parish hall. It's all still there, lurking in the shadows, and all of it singing praise to God.

One of the most astonishing things about blighted neighborhoods is how long the churches remain after the stores vanish and the housing decays. When everything else is gone, the sacred stones stand amid the rubble and the vacant lots, a testament to the prayers that live on inside the walls. Sometimes the congregations are still there, keeping the prayer alive through their worship and outreach and loving care of a sacred space. Sometimes the congregations themselves are gone, yet some unspoken pact, some wordless treaty, shields these holy places from the forces of destruction that surround them. The churches are alive in the midst of death. Their very presence shouts to the heavens.

You are the steward of such a temple. If all the parishioners were silent, the stones should still cry out "Hosanna!" to their Creator. Whether they will be in any condition to do so is largely up to you.

Whoever does the will of God is my brother and sister and mother

Mark 3:31-34

Many vestries spend a lot of time promoting family values, by which I mean creating facilities and promoting programs that will make their parishes attractive to that most desirable of all ecclesiastical demographic groups: families with young children. How to bring such families in and how to keep them coming are subjects that consume endless hours at vestry meetings, as well as a substantial portion of the annual budget in most congregations.

There's nothing wrong with trying to attract families; it's a worthy institutional goal. But the vestry has to keep that goal in perspective. Jesus, it seems, embraced a peculiar set of family values. Oh, he loved going to weddings and playing with children. But his concept of family had nothing to do with the one being promoted by certain preachers and politicians today.

The scene in the third chapter of Mark's Gospel is instructive. Jesus is speaking to a crowd when he is approached by the people he ought to value the most— his mother, whom tradition tells us he revered, and his brothers. They are concerned about him. They have heard some alarming rumors about faith healings and casting out devils and the like. They want to talk to him, to make sure he's all right. But he refuses to see them.

In fact, he won't even acknowledge that his blood kin have some special call on him. "Who are my mother and my brothers?" he asks (Mark 3:33). And looking at the crowd that was lapping up every word he had to say, he announced, "Here are my mother and my brothers! Whoever does the will of God is my brother and sister and mother" (Mark 3:34-35).

The gospel editor does well to throw an exclamation point into that statement, for it is indeed radical. Many of our churches are so busy catering to the inward-looking nuclear family that they forget that Jesus embraced a much broader type of family—one that started as a rag-tag ruffian band and eventually expanded to include the poor and every sort of social outcast, from lepers and prostitutes to Samaritans and Romans. His goal was the creation of a far-flung family bound together not by genes but by faith, caring for one another simply because of their common humanity. If we are his people, then we must let Jesus' family values rather than today's politically popular family values guide us in setting the parish agenda.

At first blush, a strong outreach program may not seem like the best way to attract those demographically desirable young families. Young adults are primarily concerned about religious education for the children; they want a good Sunday school for the young ones and a youth group for the teenagers, and generally some music to boot.

But what is religious education about if not teaching our young people to incorporate the values of Jesus in their everyday lives? Those values are the essence of Christianity, and learning them is far more important than memorizing the books of the Bible. Fortunately, in the parish outreach house there are many classrooms for teaching Jesus' family values. Little hands can help make sandwiches for the homeless. The children's choir would be welcomed at the neighborhood home for the elderly. Many outreach activities provide welcome opportunities for parents and children to serve the least of our brethren together; that's quality time at its best. And the money you budget for books and toys to furnish an inner-city day-care center represents a contribution from your children to the body of Christ.

Will some young families fail to respond to your emphasis on Jesus' family values? Will they prefer the church with the new playground equipment and the Dolby sound system? Sure they will. But the ones who will be drawn to your parish are the ones who are responding to the real Christian message. They are about as desirable an addition to your parish family as I can imagine.

Do business with these until I come back

Luke 19:12-26

I've always thought that the Bible story most relevant to the work of a vestry is the parable of the talents. Everything about it speaks to where you find yourselves. The three leading characters are stewards, just as you are. Their master entrusts his worldly goods to them, just as God and your congregation have entrusted the parish's worldly goods to you. To one steward the master gives much. To another he gives more modestly. And to yet another he gives very little. Like the stewards, different vestries find themselves with different asset levels. But how much anyone receives is irrelevant; the master expects each steward to make more of whatever was entrusted to him. Of course the master is a hard man, so the stewards dare not be careless with his wealth. But it is not sufficient to preserve what was given. The good steward must find a way to make it grow.

Some parishes are fortunate to have some sort of endowment, and most parishes receive bequests or special contributions from time to time. Vestry members would do well to examine their attitudes about the stewardship of such moneys in light of the parable of the talents. There are lessons to be learned.

To paraphrase what football coach Woody Hayes once said about the forward pass, there are three things that vestry members can do with endowments and special contributions, and two of them are bad. The first is to spend those moneys in ways that will not help the congregation grow in size or in faith. If a parish is living beyond its means, so that it has to dip into the endowment or use a timely bequest to balance the budget, the vestry cannot possibly make more of the talents entrusted to it.

The second common error is to hoard the bank account and refuse to spend it at all. This is not just silly; it is fiscally imprudent. In the workaday world there is a well-known maxim: You have to spend money to make money. That means you have to invest in order to increase your assets.

Well, it works the same way in churches. The parishes that attract new members—and end up with more to spend in the long run—are the ones that make careful investments to turn themselves into vibrant, caring communities. They don't use endowment or special gifts to pay the fuel bill, but they don't bury them in the bank either. Instead, they add or improve an educational program. They develop new and appealing outreach efforts or an after-school center or a community theater. They make sure that the doors are open on days other than Sunday, and that members and non-members alike have a reason to drop by. People hear about that, and they get curious about just who and what that church might be. You may recall the catch phrase from a recent movie: "If you build it, they will come." The movie was right.

The rationale for hanging onto parish funds is that they will be available for a rainy day. I'm not suggesting that prudence is a vice—far from it. But Jesus made it quite clear that earning interest from a bank would not merit the accolade, "Well done, thou good and faithful servant." That's probably because Jesus knew that *every* day is a rainy day. There are people who hunger for something they can't quite put their finger on *today*, and hungry families that need to be fed *today*, and children who need to learn values *today*. The church that will not invest in order to address those needs *today* is already standing in a downpour without an umbrella.

This doesn't just go for unspent money; it applies equally to unused space and wasted abilities. All these things are our talents, and God will call us to account for how we invest them.

There's an interesting twist to the parable of the talents. The two stewards who took a prudent risk succeeded and were amply rewarded. Only the one who was afraid to try was accounted a failure. God really does help those who help themselves.

Who would build without counting the cost?
Luke 14:27-33

My husband and I are reconfiguring our top floor to accommodate two boys and one scarlet macaw. It's not an extensive renovation, but it took a lot of planning, in terms of design and timing and budget, and even special considerations like the fact that one of the boys is allergic to the bird. We didn't start until we had thought everything through, and we rejected a lot of perfectly sound ideas because they wouldn't meet our needs or would cost too much. We did not begin our project until we were convinced that we had found the most cost-effective way to solve our space problem.

Most vestries need to build from time to time. Sometimes they build literally, by replacing the roof or converting part of the parish hall into classroom space. And sometimes they build figuratively, by expanding the music program or committing to a new outreach ministry. Either way, the goal is the same: to adapt the parish to the changing needs of the congregation and community. And either way, the vestry needs to assess the cost before beginning.

It's easy to remember Jesus' admonition to count the cost before we start building when we're talking about construction in the hard-hat sense. I have never met a vestry member who failed to act like a good steward when confronted with a proposal to renovate the church buildings.

But what about those other types of building that vestries are asked to support? They, too, carry a cost. Sometimes that cost can be measured in dollars and cents: More religious education, for instance, requires additional materials or classrooms or lecturers or even a coordinator. But sometimes the cost is harder to discern and measure. Will expanding classroom space mean that the Boy Scouts and Alcoholics Anonymous can no longer meet on your site? If so, how will that alter your profile in the community? Can the sexton handle increased use of space on his current budget? Will one of your bright ideas for growth or outreach create such ill will that even a modest financial cost is simply too great?

My own parish recently had to count this sort of cost in a very painful way. We house a nursery school for very young children in our parish house. For some years, the school has wanted a playground. We are woefully short of outdoor space, but a creative architect designed a small, fenced-in play yard to fit into one corner of our beautiful columbarium garden. Many in the parish warmed to the thought of baby laughter floating over the memorial stones. But dozens of others, including people who had interred loved ones in the columbarium, felt differently. In the end, the project was abandoned, not because it made no sense or cost too much money, but because it would have hurt too many feelings. No vestry should ever build without counting *that* cost.

There is another type of cost you might count before saying yes or no to a project: the cost of not going ahead. There's always someone who will find something to complain about when change of any sort is proposed. Sometimes the ones who complain the loudest will be valued members of your congregation, and you will be understandably loath to offend them. But there can be no growth without change. If you refuse to support new ideas just because some voices are raised in dissent, your congregation will inevitably find itself on a downward trajectory. Sometimes a vestry needs to build on an idea that holds out the promise of new life, even if it means that a few will refuse to follow where you lead.

In all events, the most foolish course of all is to rush willy-nilly into something new without weighing all the options. Much of what you do as a vestry is devoted to raising up and pointing out the relative costs and benefits of parish proposals. Whether you conclude that the cost is justified or not, you will have discharged your duty by counting it.

For the task is too heavy for you; you cannot do it alone

Exodus 18:13-27

If you think of the Israelites as a congregation, Moses as its first pastor, and the council of elders as the first vestry, you can learn three important lessons from this passage.

First, even a miracle man can't do everything. The Israelites expected Moses to take care of them. It was a logical expectation. After all, he had broken the Egyptians, led his people out of slavery, and found them food and water in a desert. But as his father-in-law saw all too clearly (no doubt after a chat with the neglected Mrs. Moses), letting Moses do it all wasn't working. Things were left undone, and Moses was a wreck.

American churchgoers have been socialized to expect that the minister will do all the ministering, but that's impossible. It leads to overwork and burnout. At best, things don't get done well; at worst, they don't get done at all. The welfare of the congregation and the welfare of the priest suffer. The model is no good. It had to change for Israel, and it has to change for us.

Second, someone had to sit Moses down and tell him that he couldn't do it all. Three thousand years later, nothing has changed. I don't know what it is about priests, but many of them seem to have internalized the erroneous idea that they have to do everything themselves. They pay lip service to sharing responsibility, but when push comes to shove, they are reluctant to share any of theirs. I remember one overworked cleric who talked the talk of sharing ministry with his parishioners but didn't walk the walk. Worried about his increasing exhaustion, the vestry suggested organizing a lay group to make hospital calls. In his typically harried way, the rector explained that he couldn't possibly accept this well-intentioned proposal. "People want to see the rector at the hospital," he said. True enough, but with the press of work, it wasn't always possible for him to go. The result: Days would pass without anyone visiting. The sick person, who just wanted to see someone, felt neglected. The priest, who didn't want to let anyone down, felt guilty. And the vestry, which only wanted to help, felt useless. It was frustration all around.

"It's the priest's job" is a recipe for disaster today, just as it was in the wilderness. Fortunately for Moses, Israel, and world history, Jethro cared enough to point out that the audience was not clapping for Moses' one-man show. He suggested that Moses pick some helpers and let them help govern the people. The solution seems so obvious. Still, I imagine that Moses did not leap at Jethro's suggestion. Sharing responsibility implies sharing power, and even a saint has trouble with that. But eventually, he saw that Jethro's suggestion was wise. If your priest suffers from the same sort of tunnel vision that afflicted Moses, it might be part of your ministry to be her Jethro.

Third, even with a council to help share the tasks of administration, there were some jobs only Moses could do. Jethro, who was nothing if not a clear thinker, realized that Moses could not send a substitute up the mountain to talk with God or teach his people God's law. These tasks could not be delegated. Everything else he could spread around.

With our church's renewed emphasis on the priesthood of all believers, the line between priestly and lay ministry sometimes blurs. That's not always a bad thing, but vestry members might read and reflect on the job description that the bishop reads to every new priest just before ordination (BCP, page 531). Priests are specially called to proclaim the gospel by preaching and teaching, to declare God's forgiveness for sins, to bless, to baptize, and to celebrate the Eucharist. These are the pastor's equivalent of Moses' nondelegable duties. Your job is to free enough of your priest's time so she can plan the liturgy, write the sermon, instruct the seeker, and counsel the penitent—as well as renew herself through prayer and meditation, so all those tasks are done well. By doing your job, you enable her to do what only she can. You share thereby in the teaching and blessing and feeding of the entire congregation. What a noble calling.

───── Relationships ─────

*And the apostles and elders met together to
consider the matter*

Acts 15:1-29

From our vantage point, it seems silly that the Early
Church nearly foundered over the technical issue of
whether a Gentile had to become a Jew before he could
become a Christian. Then again, to an outsider, it may
seem incredible that whatever issue is tearing your parish apart assumes such importance and engenders such
divisiveness. Difficult issues are peculiar to their time
and situation. However, that doesn't mean we can't
look to a common template for handling them. The
fifteenth chapter of the Acts of the Apostles provides
that template.

The opening sentences set out the problem. A tra-
ditionalist faction of the new Nazarene sect demanded
that new converts adhere to the Law of Moses. Those
who ministered to the Gentiles recognized that they
could kiss their fledgling congregations good-bye if
new members had to be circumcised and keep kosher.
So a party was sent to Jerusalem to obtain a definitive
ruling.

This gives us our first clue about conflict resolution in the church. We are concerned about unity, the kind of unity that Jesus wanted for his followers: "that they all may be one" (John 17:21). So we try to discern God's will *corporately*. We are not meant to "turn every one to his own way" (Isaiah 53:4-6). Paul and Barnabas were pretty clear in their own minds about the right answer, but rather than impose their position by fiat—and rupture the fledgling community in the process—they trusted the Spirit to work through the assembled people of God. As a friend of mine used to say, that's good process. So good, in fact, that we have actually written it into our church's framework. Because we value corporate discernment and consensus, we elect a vestry—a group of leaders—rather than install an autocrat at the helm.

When the delegation reached Jerusalem, Acts tells us that there was "much debate" (Acts 15:7). Corporate discernment requires broad consultation and frank discussion of all points of view. In a time of controversy, it's rarely advisable for the vestry to play it too close to the vest. Set out the issue, and let the rest of the congregation tell you what they think. Encourage everyone to make their opinions known and to point out, in a Christian way, any flaws they see in the opposing view.

After the debate had aired for a while, Peter, Paul, and Barnabas recounted what had happened when they dispensed Jesus' message to the Gentiles. They suggested that the fruit of their labor was the best possible proof of God's will. The testimony of people with experience obviously carried great weight, since theirs are the only statements quoted by the author of Acts. Experience is often the best teacher, and a wise assembly will pay special attention to the views of people who can back up their opinions with evidence from their own lives.

There came a point back in Jerusalem when "the whole assembly kept silence, and listened" (Acts 15:12). A period of silent reflection lets you, the leadership, assimilate the various points of view you have heard and try to make sense of it all. It also affords an opportunity for prayer. A vestry *can* act without praying, but it is surely the better practice to sit awhile and listen for the still, small voice that is the surest guide to right action.

Finally, James, who qualifies as the first senior warden, rose and put a motion to the assembly. He didn't follow Robert's Rules of Order, but he set forth what seemed the best position and obtained "the consent of the whole church" (Acts 15:22) to carry it out. Of course, we no longer act by assembly; your congregation elected you to make decisions on its behalf. Once you have everyone's input, including God's, you do what seems best. Perhaps there will be dissenters. It's likely that a few members of the pharisaic party quit the church in disgust after James's motion was adopted. But we never hear about them again, which suggests that their objections ceased to be important once the church had done its best to find God's way.

The decision-making process outlined in the fifteenth chapter of Acts may be two thousand years old, but nothing tried in the interval has worked better. You could do worse than model your own deliberations on it.

Would that all the LORD's *people were prophets!*

Numbers 11:24-30

It is a sad but true fact that most vestry members think they have to do it all: oversee the finances, chair the committees, run the programs. This kind of thinking is unfortunate. A do-it-all vestry tends to become a secret society—a clique or an in-crowd—within the parish. Nothing could be more destructive for your life as a community. Once members of the congregation get the impression that they are outsiders or unimportant, or that their opinions and ideas are not valued, they become less supportive of the church. Then the vestry *will* have to do everything.

If you should find yourselves drifting into the sort of thought pattern that leads to the in-crowd mentality, you might want to remember the story of Eldad and Medad. When Moses chose certain Hebrew elders to help him govern Israel, Eldad and Medad were not among them. These two worthies remained back in the camp while Moses took seventy others—carefully selected leaders, every one of them—to the Tent of the Meeting. There the elect received a share of the Spirit. As a sign of their special calling, they fell into a one-time prophetic frenzy.

But when Moses and the seventy returned to camp, they found a frenzied Eldad and Medad prophesying away. Although not chosen for leadership, these two were obviously filled with every bit as much Spirit as those selected by Moses to be his vestry. Joshua, Moses' second in command and one of the elect, did not like this development one bit, probably because he had been feeling really special about being among the chosen few. He got quite huffy and said to Moses, "Lord, stop them!" Moses, however, was in tune with the mind of God. He knew that the Spirit blows where it will. If the Lord God wanted Eldad and Medad to prophesy on his behalf, neither Moses nor Joshua nor anyone else could stop it. So he chastised Joshua, "Are you jealous on my account? Would that all the LORD's people were prophets, and that the LORD would put his Spirit upon them!" (Num. 11:29).

Moses knew whereof he spoke. Through an election, you are on the vestry, but through God's baptismal election, every member of your parish has received a share of the Spirit and the authority to act for God in this world. Vestries that keep all the work for themselves are guilty of bad theology and bad stewardship—bad theology because all the baptized have been elected to do the Lord's work, and bad stewardship because it's a waste of the parish's human resources, which have been entrusted to your care. Part of your task as stewards is to encourage everyone in your congregation to do the work of the parish together with you. In some parishes, it's tough to find people who are willing to spend part of their spare time tending to church business. But in most congregations, there are plenty of people who would be willing to serve in some capacity, even if they aren't members of the vestry.

Jesus himself demonstrated that using everyone to get his message out was the way to go. He selected twelve men to be his closest companions and confidants, but when it came time to send out emissaries to spread the Word, he did not confine himself to so small a group. No, he sent seventy disciples on the road (Luke 10:1-11). Some of the Twelve may have felt a bit threatened by this sharing of their special status, but since the seventy "returned with joy" (Luke 10:17), I think we can safely assume that these additional ministers of the gospel were also filled with God's Spirit, just like Eldad and Medad. It is no different in your parish.

It's a lucky vestry that has a congregation full of Eldads and Medads, and a wise one that recognizes how fortunate it is that there are others who will prophesy right along with you. Treasure everyone's gifts and use them wisely.

The disagreement became so sharp that they parted company

Acts 15:36-40

During your years on the vestry, you will get to know some terrific people who would otherwise have remained nodding acquaintances on Sunday morning. You will discover facets and talents in people that you never suspected were there. You will experience the peculiar satisfaction that teamwork brings. If you are lucky, as I was, you will develop some extremely rewarding friendships. This is the upside of going on the vestry, and it's pretty up.

However, vestries are as susceptible as other groups to the pressures and behaviors that tear communities apart. Jealousy, competition, factionalism, a sense of betrayal... all that and more will surface, during meetings and in those private conversations that inevitably occur before you convene and after you've gone home. One might think working for the church would help us resist those pressures. But sometimes the very fact that we are on a godly mission causes us to become self-righteous when these unchristian behaviors surface. And self-righteousness is the first step on the path to a vestry that falls apart. Just look at what happened to Paul and Barnabas.

There's no denying that Paul was one of the Lord's hardest and most effective workers. However, he could be extremely self-righteous (just read one or two of his Epistles and see if you don't agree). It tripped him up from time to time. One of the saddest moments in the New Testament comes at the end of the fifteenth chapter of the Acts of the Apostles. After years of hard work abroad, Paul and his long-time companion, Barnabas, had just scored their greatest triumph. The leaders of the church in Jerusalem, impressed by their results, had decided that Gentile converts need not embrace Judaism in order to be fully accepted by the Way (as the new movement was known). Back out on the road they went, thrilled with the news they were bringing to their fledgling congregations, and full of renewed zeal for their mission—until Barnabas wanted to take a young fellow named John Mark on their travels. John Mark had somehow deserted them in the past, and Paul, smarting over this inadequacy, got his back up and refused to accept him. The boy was unworthy, and that was that. Forget about tolerance and human undeserving and forgiveness and second chances, and all the rest of what Jesus had to say on that score. Paul, the self-righteous disciple, was not about to give John Mark another opportunity to prove himself. So what happened? "The disagreement became so sharp" the author tells us, "that they parted company" (Acts 15:39). In other words, Paul broke up the best missionary team in history just to prove that he was right.

Every vestry has room for people with strong opinions, people who will fight for ideas they believe in. No vestry has room for people who are so confident about their own views that they will not try to find the merit in someone else's. You may think you know how best to respond to some situation facing your parish, and you may well be right. But when being right slides into being self-righteous, it will probably become a destructive force within your group. People who become totally convinced about their point of view start to solicit allies, which leads to folks choosing sides, which leads to the formation of factions within what ought to be a cohesive body. Factionalism only emphasizes our differences and makes them harder to resolve.

Paul may or may not have been right about John Mark's missionary abilities, but he was wrong to get so carried away by his own point of view that he tore his team apart. If you make the same mistake, if you get so carried away by your own rectitude that you end up generating heat, not light, you could end up tearing your vestry apart and frittering away what your parish has entrusted to you. Is your point of view worth such divisiveness?

When you are offering your gift at the altar, if you remember that your brother has something against you...

Matthew 5:21-24

The day will probably come when you will have a terrible fight with another member of the vestry. You will storm out of your meeting angry and frustrated. Your head will be sore, and so will your hand, because you will hit a wall after you get home. You'll toss and turn all night. You know you'll never be able to work with that idiot again.

A few days later Sunday will dawn. You will roll out of bed and into a pew. Your nemesis will be sitting a few rows away. You'll want to punch him out, but instead you will arch your eyebrows and give him a barely perceptible nod. He will do the same. And both of you will mentally congratulate yourself for your civilized and absolutely correct behavior.

You will kneel down and open the Prayer Book, expecting that Sunday morning calm to descend, but the words won't make sense. Or you'll try to say your prayers, only they won't come out right. The peace of the Lord that passeth understanding passeth you right by, and every time you glance across the aisle, you know why.

What do you do now?

Jesus was pretty explicit about this one. "When you are offering your gift at the altar, if you remember that your brother or sister has something against you, leave

your gift there before the altar and go; first be reconciled
to your brother or sister, and then come and offer your
gift" (Mt. 5:23-24). If we live by the gospel, we can't hold
grudges for long. For those of us who attend church
every Sunday, six days is absolutely the outer limit of
what we get. Usually it's less. Then we have to make sure
we are fit to approach the altar, so we can offer the gift of
ourselves to the God who made us for himself.

What Jesus asks—that we lay aside our pride and
self-righteousness and reconcile—is hard, particularly
when the other person is in the wrong, or when whatever happened is really not our fault. But the business of
the vestry can't be done in an atmosphere of anger and
resentment. As John the Epistoler reminds us, anyone
who hates another believer is in the darkness and does
not know the way to go (1 Jn. 2:11). I don't know about
you, but I don't care to entrust the affairs of my parish
to folks who don't know where they are going.

So you need a way out. Well, what do you do when
you want to make up with someone after a tiff, or to
straighten out a misunderstanding? I often sit down over
lunch, a cup of coffee, or a drink. For some reason I've
never been able to figure out, it's easier to iron things
out over a meal. Conversely, it's all but impossible to
eat with someone you're mad at; you practically have to
choke down the food.

Whenever you come to church, you are invited
to the table. The Eucharist is God's own version of a

reconciling meal, and when received in the right spirit, is even more effective at breaking down resentments and smoothing things over.

When we receive Communion in my parish, we kneel before a magnificent wooden carving of the Last Supper. Jesus stands at the center. He is extending his hands toward the bread on his left and the cup on his right, ready to pass them around to his friends. If you reached out while kneeling at the rail, you could just about grab one of those outstretched hands. If your nemesis grabbed the other, Jesus would be a bridge between you. And the grace of the sacrament, which you are both receiving, would spill from each of you to the other.

You probably don't have a reredos like mine over your altar. But if you fix that image in your mind, and imagine Jesus reaching out his hands to both of you over the table, I'm sure it will do the trick. Jesus, the giver of the feast, can bridge over the distance between us. He is the common ground where reconciliation lies. If you reach for him, you will find it.

———— Prayer ————

They proposed two... Then they prayed and said, "Lord... show us which one of these two you have chosen"

Acts 1:15-26

The first critical decision for the leaders of the Early Church was how to replace Judas. After Peter convinced his brethren that they really should be twelve rather than eleven, they proposed two candidates—both men "who have accompanied us during all the time that the Lord Jesus went in and out among us" (Acts 1:21)—and they devised a method for choosing: They drew lots. Then, before making the choice, they prayed about it. They asked God to guide the choice.

Nothing is more important to vestries and their members than prayer. Yet many vestries limit their communal prayer to a brief invocation at the beginning of each meeting and "Go in peace to love and serve the Lord" at the end. And few parishes emphasize the importance of private prayer to effective vestry service.

Big mistake. The vestries that work the best pray a lot. I know it sounds hokey, but it's really true that the vestry that prays together stays together.

Consider gathering fifteen to thirty minutes prior to the business portion of the meeting for prayer and meditation. I say "prior to the business portion of the meeting" rather than "prior to the meeting" because corporate prayer is to be an integral part of the meeting, not something you can skip and still make it to the main event. Since God is the added dimension that makes serving on the vestry different from belonging to some other board or task force, talking to God is as necessary to your work as your talents or your ideas or your commitment. If you shortchange prayer, you forget who you are and what you are about.

How you pray depends on your parish personality. If you meet in the evening, Evening Prayer offers an ideal combination of praise, thanksgiving, intercession, and Scripture for meditation. If a formal office does not appeal, try passing out a passage of Scripture or a brief written meditation when you distribute the meeting agenda, and let the members react to it. Vestries that meet after church one Sunday a month might prefer to reflect on a passage from the day's lectionary, or on the sermon. Allowing someone besides the clergy to lead a scriptural meditation can create a powerful prayer experience not only for the prayer leader but for the whole group. Some vestries spend time in "Quaker prayer," sitting in silence and waiting for inspiration; others go around the table, with each member adding to a chain of prayer.

The best prayer of all is the Eucharist. Although it is impractical for most vestries to hold a Eucharist before every meeting, nothing strengthens the bonds that are so critical to successful group ministry like gathering in table fellowship from time to time. Vestry Eucharists lend themselves to physical closeness and participation by everyone in a way that is impossible with a larger congregation, or one not united by a common task. I particularly remember several Eucharists where we gathered in a circle around the altar and passed the elements from hand to hand at Communion. The extraordinary symbolism of feeding one another was not lost on anyone in the room; we were better for it and more effective in our work.

Every vestry member needs to cultivate a personal prayer life as well. Regular public worship with the rest of the parish is vital, but a vestry member's prayer life cannot be so limited. Try to spend some time in prayer every day, with special attention to the needs of the parish. Again, how to spend that time is a deeply personal decision. Some people need the anchor of formal prayer, such as one of the Daily Offices or selections from the Prayer Book. Others prefer silent contemplation of a scriptural passage or devotional text like this one. Studying Scripture, theology, and church history can also prove inspirational. Still others recharge through centering prayer. *What* you do doesn't matter. *That* you do matters immensely.

Prayer is the source of knowledge and nourishment for the soul; both are vital if you are to succeed at your task.

Martha, Martha, you are troubled by many things

Luke 10:38-42

For most folks, going to church offers a respite from the cares of the world—a quiet place where they can breathe a little more slowly, think a little more clearly, and pray a little more reverently. They come in once a week, say hello to the usher who hands them a bulletin, take a seat, close their eyes, cross themselves, and wait for the familiar beauty of the liturgy to waft them heavenward, lost in wonder, love, and praise. They make mental comments on the sermon and the anthem, feed on bread, wine, coffee, and donuts, catch up on a little local gossip, and head home after picking up the kids at church school. So what if the plaster in the parish office is falling all over the secretary's new computer, pledges are down, and no one will volunteer for the hospitality committee. That's someone else's problem.

You, of course, know whose problem these things are—yours. You won't be in office long before every visit to the premises takes on the trappings of a business trip. You can't look up without seeing the wet spot on the ceiling, and you can't hear the music without remembering that the organist said something about needing new leather on the pistons, whatever that means. And when there's nothing else to take your attention off the Lord, rest assured that Mrs. Jones will grab your elbow to complain about what you have done and to remind you of what you have left undone.

You are Martha reincarnate, with ample reason to complain to Jesus about all those Marys out there in the pews. It's your hard work and worry that allows them to worship in bliss, isn't it? And he has the temerity to tell you that *they* have chosen the better part? Really!

Martha is a much misunderstood figure. Her problem is not that she has a job to do and does it—after all, if she did not, no one in her house would have food to eat or clean clothes to wear. Martha's problem is that she gets so carried away by her work that she can't see the obvious, which is that *the Lord has dropped in for a visit.* She's gotten so bogged down in her job that she becomes unable to set it aside for a few minutes, as Mary can, to receive the simple, beautiful grace of God's presence in her house.

Vestry members carry a lot of responsibility on their shoulders. Therefore, you are in danger of falling victim to the Martha syndrome. Remind yourselves that where God is concerned the first order of business is cultivating that relationship. Prayer is more important than fixing the roof or paying the bills. That's not to minimize the importance of the vestry's special calling; you are correct that your behind-the-scenes efforts make everything run smoothly for the weekly visitor. But by grounding your work in prayer, you will appreciate why it is so important: Doing it glorifies God. And you are less likely to burn out before your tasks are complete.

The great abbot St. Benedict made this truth the cornerstone of his monastic rule, which is still followed by many monks, nuns, and laypersons today. Benedict recognized the importance of work in the quest for spiritual perfection. At the same time, however, he insisted that physical or mental work be interrupted periodically for the more important work of prayer—which put God at the center of everything.

So when you come into your church—not just on Sunday morning, but every single time, and especially when you are about to tackle the holy work of the vestry—take a moment with Jesus to refresh yourself. After all, he was very clear: Mary, not Martha, chose the better part. Don't make the same mistake.

Come away to a deserted place all by yourselves and rest a while

Mark 6:30-33

In my parish, the rector's announcement of the vestry retreat is greeted with a level of enthusiasm usually reserved for a dose of castor oil. No one has time. Everyone suddenly finds a scheduling conflict. The thought of wasting a Friday night and all day Saturday, even once a year, on church business is more than a lot of vestry members are prepared to put up with.

You probably don't know this, but Jesus conducted the first vestry retreat. You'll find the evidence in an often overlooked passage in the Gospel of Mark that comes just before the famous story of the feeding of the five thousand. The apostles, having returned from their mission to the people of Galilee, meet with Jesus to report on what they had done and taught. Jesus finds the ambience distracting, "for many were coming and going, and they had no leisure even to eat" (Mark 6:31). So he tells his friends to come away to a deserted place where they can rest and relax and talk in depth. They climb into a boat and away they go for some private time. Voila—a vestry retreat.

I imagine that vestry retreats are almost universally unpopular. However, as Jesus started the tradition, perhaps it is worth reevaluating that view.

One common complaint about vestry retreats is that they are, or should be, unnecessary. After all, the vestry meets regularly; it ought to be able to deal with its business in the allotted time. The gospel, however, suggests otherwise. Let's reconstruct the situation. Jesus and his people, his field team, needed to reconnoiter, to hear reports from each other and discuss what the next phase of their ministry might be. But there were too many distractions and interruptions in the place where they ordinarily congregated—folks seeking cures and comfort and advice and that sort of thing. Sound familiar? Jesus decided he had to get the apostles away from all those distractions before they could work intensively. In this, as in so many things, Jesus was prescient. In our era of instant access and intrusive communications and multiple demands on everyone's time, it is increasingly necessary for groups of leaders to get away from life's everyday demands in order to discuss the past and plan for the future in a focused way. Corporate executives do it; law firms do it; sales forces do it; union officials do it. Why not vestries?

The second complaint is that retreats are boring. But if your vestry retreat is all work and no play, you are leaving out a component that Jesus considered vital. The evangelist uses an interesting phrase: "They were without *leisure*, even to eat." Apparently, it was important to Jesus that his apostles should spend some social time together, relaxing, enjoying a meal, getting to know each other as people, not just as members of the Jesus team. Down time is programmed into every management retreat because it's a cardinal rule that people will work together better if they have built camaraderie. One reason to have a vestry retreat is to provide leisure time for forging friendships and building better working relationships. You might find that you can work more efficiently during the year if you take this heaven-sent opportunity to get to know each other.

The third complaint is that the vestry retreat is "just another business meeting." It won't be if prayer is prominent on the agenda. The Gospels tell us that Jesus prayed when he escaped to deserted places, so there's every reason to assume that he used his brief getaway with the apostles to engage in some corporate prayer for their common ministry. You can use the vestry retreat for the same purpose. As custodians of your congregation's resources, you have a special obligation to keep the interests of the parish before you and God at all times. The retreat is your chance to begin cultivating the practice of praying for your parish, your clergy, the members of the congregation, and the special work of the vestry.

So before you roll your eyes and find something else to do on vestry retreat weekend, remember all the good that can come from going off to a deserted place with Jesus and the rest of your vestry friends. Then get in that boat and row away.

——————— Moving On ———————

Moses went up from the plains of Moab to Mount Nebo... and the LORD showed him the whole land

Deuteronomy 34:1-8

You'll know when it's time to leave the vestry. Maybe you'll have reached the end of your term and you'll be ineligible to re-up. Maybe you'll be moving out of the parish, or into a new job that will make too many demands on your time for awhile. Or maybe you'll just feel tired and burned out and in need of a rest. Whatever the reason, you will have a sense that it's time to go. Most probably, you will be relieved that the end of your stewardship is in sight.

But even if your prime emotion is delight, you will not be without regrets as you lay down your load. During your years on the vestry, you will have developed a vision about the future of your parish. You will have set some things in motion to make that vision a reality. You will have generated or endorsed new ideas or programs, and the jury will still be out on whether they work. Don't be surprised if you feel proprietary toward your unfinished projects and are somewhat reluctant to hand them over to anyone else—especially if you're not sure that your successor fully appreciates your wisdom.

In a continuing institution like the church, the leader's special curse is that he or she must let someone else interpret the vision and finish the job. There is a wonderful Bible passage that illustrates this curse: Moses on Mt. Nebo. At the end of his long and productive life, Moses was allowed to see the Promised Land, but though he had led his people to its borders, he could not lead them in. That was someone else's job.

At the end of your years on the vestry, you will be like Moses on Mt. Nebo. You will have seen the Promised Land and labored mightily to get there. But like Moses, you will have to let someone else lead your congregation there. That will leave you feeling mighty conflicted, no matter how much you long to give up the burden of vestry service.

I happen to think it's a good thing, in the main, that parish leaders have to let others finish the work they begin. The true test of whether a plan or a program has staying power is whether it flourishes under the next generation of leaders or dies on the vine. If an idea or project survives your departure, then you can be pretty sure that the community as a whole has taken ownership of it. On the other hand, if that idea or project can't survive unless you are there to make sure it happens, perhaps the idea was really about you and not the parish.

If passing the baton is good for the parish, it's also good for the leaders who must step aside. Too often, when we've led a congregation for a very long time, we start to equate the parish with ourselves and to believe that we're indispensable to the welfare of the congregation as a whole. There is a real spiritual danger in such attitudes: They can cause us to become so attuned to our own voice that we can't hear God's. Moreover, we are a community whose members ultimately define themselves, not in terms of leadership, but as followers—followers of the One whose primary command was "Follow me." To follow is a Christian's highest calling. If we forget that (as those who lead for too long are prone to do), we are in danger of losing touch with one of the most fundamental characteristics of Christian life.

Admittedly, this sort of thinking doesn't always lessen the frustration of having to let go of the reins of leadership. However, perhaps the next phase of your congregational life will be just as satisfying. Moses did not make it into the land flowing with milk and honey, but shortly after he came down from Ebo, God called him to another Promised Land. As you step down from this ministry, rest assured that God is calling you to go somewhere else in his service. Sit quietly and listen for that still, small voice, and you may begin to sense the possibilities for other kinds of leadership before you know it.

He had been made known to them in the breaking of the bread

Luke 24:13-35

I asked my rector one day if there were any subjects he thought I should address in this book. He immediately replied, "I hope you're doing a meditation on the need for people to recover their spirituality after they leave the vestry." Since one of the reasons I had ended my own vestry service was to get back in touch with God, I was surprised I hadn't thought of it myself.

After you spend a few years worrying about the more mundane aspects of church life—the boilers, the bills, and the brouhahas—don't be surprised if your spiritual resources are somewhat depleted. The reason is simple. We live in a society that tends to associate God and spirituality with one's parish church. But thanks to all those worldly vestry associations, your parish church may not seem as much like the holy of holies as it used to, which means it's probably not the best place to try to recover what several years of vestry service may have obscured—your relationship with God. I don't mean to suggest that you should go somewhere else—or worse yet, stop going to church altogether—while you decompress. But you may find that your spiritual life rebounds more quickly if you look for God someplace else. Where might that be?

The story of the two disciples who walked to Emmaus with a seeming stranger is one of my favorite gospel passages. I love it because of the way the sad, embittered disciples rediscovered their Lord. They did not recognize him because of his eloquence, or from the sight of his glorified body. The voice and visage of God were beyond their comprehension. Instead, they figured out who their companion was when they saw him perform a common gesture: breaking bread.

To understand why this moves me so, you have to know that many meals in a devout Jewish home are preceded by a prayer called the *ha'motzi*, or the blessing of the bread. The leader recites a traditional prayer of thanksgiving over a loaf ("Blessed art thou, O Lord God, King of the universe, who has given us this bread to eat"), breaks the bread, and passes it to all the diners, so everyone can share a bite. This is the Jewish version of saying grace. Jesus and his contemporaries must have done it thousands of times. In fact, Jesus instituted the Eucharist while saying the Passover *ha'motzi* at the Last Supper (he gave thanks, broke the bread, and passed it around the table). So that night in Emmaus, the unrecognized stranger did nothing startling, nothing out of the ordinary. He wasn't performing the equivalent of some early Christian secret handshake. No, the disciples recognized him in one of life's utterly commonplace moments.

What's the lesson that a vestry refugee can draw from this story? Well, since it will probably take awhile before you can stop agitating over your congregation's problems and feel God within the four walls of your church, look for God in the stuff of your everyday life. Who has not awakened on an exceptionally beautiful morning and basked in a feeling of contentment? Or warmed to the smile of the lady behind the checkout counter? Everyone has felt that sudden rush of love for someone special, or the satisfaction that comes with completing a task, or the joy that wells up inside us whenever the world seems more wonderful than anything could possibly be. God is in all those things. In fact, God can be found in everyone and everything, if only we are open to the possibility of an encounter.

The motto of the Society of Jesus is "finding God in all things." It is a wonderful motto, and you don't have to be a Jesuit to adopt it. The end of your tenure on the vestry is the perfect time to grasp a truth that eludes all too many Christians: God is not just in church; God is in life and is life. So don't despair if going to church is not the transcendent experience it was B.V.—Before Vestry. Look around you—and rediscover God.

Go therefore and make disciples of all nations... and teaching them to obey everything that I have commanded you
Matthew 28:19-20

Whether they leave the vestry with glee or with regret, most people feel that they have grown in God as a result of vestry service. I hope you will too. How can you integrate that into the rest of your life, both as a member of your parish and in the wider world?

Most Christians subscribe to a very narrow definition of the term *lay ministry*. We would define it as something people do for their parish church, like being on the vestry, singing in the choir, or teaching Sunday school.

But if we confine our concept of ministry to what goes on in and around a house of worship, we limit the reach of our baptismal covenant. Being a Christian is not a hobby to be indulged on Sundays and occasional evenings. It is our *vocation* to be Christians. The Great Commission at the end of Matthew's Gospel means that all of us are to spread the gospel. Since we are not all called to be street preachers, lay ministry cannot be divorced from our everyday affairs.

The best and surest way to carry the gospel to the rest of the world is for us to live out our faith in our homes, at our jobs, and in our communities. What can we do in each of these places to image some aspect of

73

God's relationship to humankind? Start with your job. For those who are in the so-called service sector, or the helping professions, the answer is pretty obvious. A doctor or nurse can readily envision her hands as an extension of those of the Great Healer. The teacher's dedication to his most difficult pupils mirrors Jesus' patience with his wooden-headed, uncomprehending disciples. Counselors offer a needed shoulder to cry on, just as the Father comforted his Son in prayer. As a judge, I can only aspire to the model of the One who offers justice tempered with mercy.

Even if your job is not service oriented, you can image God by the way you do your work. My friend Pierre Wolff, a noted Ignatian retreat master, used to direct a group of French civil engineers who were interested in transforming their work into ministry. By focusing their attention on the need for care and the primacy of public safety over other concerns, they came to understand their role as instruments of God's loving care for all people. A waiter's efficiency, a receptionist's friendly welcome, a supervisor's careful mentoring—all can transform secular work into Christian witness.

Then there is your home. Your relations with family and friends offer untold opportunities for imitating Christ. Jesus lavished loving attention on those closest to him: He taught them, comforted them, provided for them, forgave them, and supported them in their work. If you have never thought about caring for, supporting, teaching, and forgiving your spouse, children, parents, or close companions as ministry, think again.

Many worthwhile community activities that are not associated with church offer opportunities to seek and serve Christ in strangers. Tutoring programs, community fund drives, the Parent-Teacher Association—these activities may not be religious in origin, but all that is required to transform them into ministry is a new attitude on your part.

Of all the traditional forms of lay ministry that one can do around the parish, serving on the vestry—taking care of the secular side of life for God's community—is probably best suited to teaching the lesson that everything we do in this world can be a ministry if it's done for the honor and glory of God. Now is the time for you to go out into the world and apply that lesson to your own life.

I will, with God's help
Book of Common Prayer, Baptismal Service, 304-5

We Episcopalians are a very ceremonial people. Punctuating the Book of Common Prayer and the Service of Occasional Offices are various rites of welcome, investiture, and commissioning for just about everything, including being on the vestry. All of them are modeled, more or less, on the first and most important such ceremony, Holy Baptism, where we are asked if we will faithfully discharge the ministry of being Christians. We reply, "I will, with God's help." That response is at once a powerful proclamation of our determination to be doers and a humble acknowledgment that we need to rely on God's providence to get anything done.

Unfortunately, we do not have a rite to decommission someone who has concluded a ministry. That's a critical omission. By the time you conclude your vestry term, you have generally acquired a certain degree of ownership over your status and your work, and you may be loath to step aside. A formal farewell to vestry service, especially one that vows reliance on God's holy grace as you move on, might help you to let go.

I have taken the liberty of writing a short decommissioning ceremony for retiring vestry members. It combines a well-deserved pat on the back with a few new and very important commitments on your part. It will be harder to keep these promises than you might think. Believe me, I know: I think I violated most of them in my first year off the vestry. It will help if you ask for God's assistance. But you can do it—and you will, with God's help.

Leader: N, you were called by the people of God, to serve them as a member of the vestry of this parish. You answered their call. You have been faithful in attendance at meetings. You have been a responsible steward of the congregation's resources. You have considered our future course and your views have informed our planning. You have led by example, especially in attendance at worship and in sharing your time, talent, and treasure with Christ's church. Now, others must step forward to take your place among the leaders of this congregation. As you leave the vestry, we thank you for your service, saying with Jesus, "Well done, thou good and faithful servant." We offer you our prayers and our support as you move on in the service of our Lord, Jesus Christ. And we ask you to reaffirm your commitment to this parish as a fitting capstone to the duty you have so faithfully discharged.

N, do you reaffirm your commitment as a member of this congregation?

Member: I do.

Leader: Will you seek new ways to serve Christ in his church?

Member: I will, with God's help.

Leader: Will you continue to support the work of this parish with your time, talent, and treasure?

Member: I will, with God's help.

Leader: Will you refrain from meddling, and offer advice and counsel to the next vestry only when asked?

Member: I will, with God's help.

Leader: Will you reject gossip and backbiting about your successors, and respect the integrity of their efforts?

Member: I will, with God's help.

Leader: Will you respect the confidentiality of the new vestry's deliberations, and be content to learn about such matters when the rest of the parish does?

Member: I will, with God's help.

Leader: Will you keep confidential those matters that were entrusted to you in confidence during your tenure on the vestry?

Member: I will, with God's help.

Leader: Will you trust the Spirit to work through our newly elected leaders to guide this parish and all its members in their life and work?

Member: I will, with God's help.

Leader: Will you continue to pray for this parish, its members, its clergy, and its vestry?

Member: I will, with God's help.

Leader: O God, who sent your Son to show us that the last shall be first and that the one who would be greatest must be the least, help your servant N, who has been a faithful member of the vestry of this parish, find new ways to exercise ministry and leadership in your church. Help him/her to keep the promises made here today before you. Grant that he/she, free from the burdens of this office, might discover anew the joy of our Christian faith. Inspire him/her to be supportive of and helpful to those who take his/her place on the vestry. And grant that he/she, along with all good and faithful stewards within your kingdom, may enter into your joy, in this life and in the life hereafter. Through Jesus Christ our Lord, Amen.

www.ingramcontent.com/pod-product-compliance
Lightning Source LLC
Jackson TN
JSHW011406130125
77033JS00023B/870

*9 7 8 0 8 1 9 2 1 7 8 9 9 *